THROUGH
THEIR EYES

POEMS FROM THE HEART

Edited By Roseanna Caswell

First published in Great Britain in 2024 by:

Young Writers
Remus House
Coltsfoot Drive
Peterborough
PE2 9BF
Telephone: 01733 890066
Website: www.youngwriters.co.uk

All Rights Reserved
Book Design by Ashley Janson
© Copyright Contributors 2024
Softback ISBN 978-1-83565-847-5
Printed and bound in the UK by BookPrintingUK
Website: www.bookprintinguk.com
YB0607GZ

FOREWORD

Since 1991, here at Young Writers we have celebrated the awesome power of creative writing, especially in young adults, where it can serve as a vital method of expressing strong (and sometimes difficult) emotions, a conduit to develop empathy, and a safe, non-judgemental place to explore one's own place in the world. With every poem we see the effort and thought that each pupil published in this book has put into their work and by creating this anthology we hope to encourage them further with the ultimate goal of sparking a life-long love of writing.

Through Their Eyes challenged young writers to open their minds and pen bold, powerful poems from the points-of-view of any person or concept they could imagine – from celebrities and politicians to animals and inanimate objects, or even just to give us a glimpse of the world as they experience it. The result is this fierce collection of poetry that by turns questions injustice, imagines the innermost thoughts of influential figures or simply has fun.

The nature of the topic means that contentious or controversial figures may have been chosen as the narrators, and as such some poems may contain views or thoughts that, although may represent those of the person being written about, by no means reflect the opinions or feelings of either the author or us here at Young Writers.

We encourage young writers to express themselves and address subjects that matter to them, which sometimes means writing about sensitive or difficult topics. If you have been affected by any issues raised in this book, details on where to find help can be found at www.youngwriters.co.uk/contact-lines

CONTENTS

Banovallum School, Horncastle

Audrey Robinson-Hall (14)	1
Oliver Bushell (13)	2
Summer Shiel (13)	4
Jessie Pearson (15)	6
Daisy-May Simpson (12)	8
Evie Ladlow (13)	9
Tabitha Cameron (15)	10
Eva Raimondo (11)	11
Libby Harness (12)	12
Caitlin Barnes (14)	13
Dylan Hillier (15)	14
Mariama Egan (15)	15
Coen Warren (15)	16
Henry Williams (12)	17
Priya Bennett (12)	18
Ellie Burge (14)	19
Bella Webster (12)	20
Amelia Hennessy (12)	21
Evie Booth (14)	22
Skye Bown (14)	23
Megan Patnell	24
Madeline Yates (12)	25
Arran Giffen (13)	26
Lily-Mai Garner-Jones (12) & Kiara Ross (12)	27
Paige Harrison (13)	28
Olivia Midgley (14)	29
Jake Steele (12)	30
Liam Jones	31
Toby Rawdon (12)	32
Harriet Gleeson (12)	33
George Hickling (12)	34
Archie Fincham	35
Faith Fenwick (15)	36
Alice Skayman (13)	37
Leah Walls (15)	38
Noah Sim (12)	39
Bella Evans (13)	40

Grove Academy, Slough

Lovepreet Singh (14)	41
Ahmed Tarar (14)	42
Leonie Ward (15)	44
Lara Costa (14)	45
Ashley S (12)	46
Aurora Sahiti (15)	48
Kacper Kowalenko (15)	49
Vanessa Pereira (14)	50
Cristian Georgescu (15)	51
Natalia Brodowicz (13)	52
Princess Chantelle Zivurawa (14)	53
Floria Sony (15)	54
Szymonek C (14)	55
Koshin Aweys (13)	56
Sanjana Sree Rajaram (14)	57
Betjina Rebelo (14)	58
Elvis Nkongo (14)	59
Moroyinmola Ogundimu (13) & Bihter	60
Ibrahim Ahmer (12)	61

King Edward VI Handsworth School For Girls, Handsworth

Japji Kaur	62

Maricourt Catholic High School, Liverpool

Eva Donoghue (14)	63
Zuha Irfan (13)	64
Hannah Robinson (15)	66

Ponteland High School, Ponteland

Abbie Stokes (14)	68
Kate Massie (14)	70
Joseph Harrington (14)	71
Skye Rutherford (13)	72
Miles Lunn (14)	73
Ibrahim Choudhary (14)	74
Will Alderson (13)	75

Reddam House Berkshire, Wokingham

Joseph Pringle (12)	76
Saanvi Sharma (12)	78
Zoe Macbeth (11)	80
Hongyi Hu (11)	82
Oliver Thompson (11)	84
Josh Jain (12)	86
Daniel Marston (11)	87
Ahria Modi (11)	88
Andy Fang (11)	90
Benjamin Wand (12)	92
Tobi Okanlawon (12)	94
Daniela Passov (12)	95
Owen Storrie (12)	96
Poppy White (11)	97
Ritvika Anandhakrishnan (12)	98

Rushey Mead Academy, Leicester

Diya Odedra (12)	99
Zara Jamal (13)	100
Kecy Jignesh (12)	102
Jai Kukadia (12)	104
Yashvi Chauhan	105
Riya Maniz Carsane	106
Dharmik Vipulbharti	108

Ava Chohan (12)	109
Vaishnavi Purohit	110
Tejvir Singh (12)	112
Reshmi Umasutharshan	113
Hibba Nawfar (12)	114
Aaminah Mussa (12)	115

Sawston Village College, Sawston

Sasha Glushkova (11)	116
Olivia Sayers (12)	119
Mariam Boucetta (12)	120
Timur Vedernikov (12)	122
Elizabeth Hull (16)	124
Sterlin Sajan (15)	125

Swanmore College, Swanmore

Esmee Rowe	126
Eden O'Dwyer (12)	127
Georgina Stafford (12)	128
Wills Illman (13)	129
Natalie Hadfield (13)	130
Lucy Barnes (13)	131
Eve Shuker (12)	132
Daisy Edwards (13)	133
Fred Jarman (12)	134
Ella Harrison (13)	136
Henry Ainsworth (13)	138
Jack Cornwell	139
Teddy Turner	140
Erin Wade (13)	141
Chloe Pollard (14)	142
Evie Cornwell	143
Rosie Smith (12)	144
Beth Ashford	145
Molly Creese (13)	146
Olivia Evans (13)	147
William Cloud (13)	148
Emmy Mooney (12)	149
Yesya Shyshlevska (11)	150
Emily Berrow (12)	151
Seren Anthony (12)	152
Lewis Carter (12)	153

Lily Ashman (12)	154
Lilly	155
Georgia April (13)	156
Taylor Oosthuizen (12)	157
Caitlin-Rose Rappini	158
Evie Carter (12)	159
Mariella Osborne (12)	160
Jessi Bicknelle-Kendall (13)	161
Arthur Naysmith (11)	162
Thomas Oates (12)	163
Hayden Buckman (12)	164
Noah Sumner (12)	165
Ruby Webb	166
Annabel Phillips (12)	167
Eva Bowyer (12)	168
Teagan Callaghan (13)	169
Tessa Adkins (12)	170
Abigail Wilkinson (12)	171
Scarlett Beech (12)	172
Mia Thomas (13)	173
Thomas Grealy (13)	174
Delilah Hatcher	175
Theo Southall	176
Harry Teague (13)	177
Isabelle Booth (12)	178
Wilfred Hammond (13)	179
Matilda Horn (13)	180
Seth Henderson (11)	181
Ezri Hosking (12)	182

The Commonweal School, Swindon

Emily Pidduck	183
Molly Sargent (11)	184

Waterloo Lodge School, Chorley

Luke Ireland (14)	187
Hayleigh Carlos (15)	188
Jessica Hinton (15)	189

THE POEMS

Everyday Mobile Phone

20:58, 20:59, 21:00... The clock in the corner of my mind ticks by the minutes.
40%, 39%, 38%... My battery slowly dwindling and gradually dying.
The endless prodding of fingers and thumbs feel like pin-pricks.
Still working, keep going, load, load, faster, faster...
I'm trying.

New message from Mum: 'Hey honey, what time are you going to get home?'
New notification from shopping website: 'We value you as a customer, buy our new product!'
Ignore. Select: 'We have a special deal for you!'
'Please, honey, pick up the phone'.
Scroll through my pages of propaganda, filter out important messages like they're just muck.

You cradle me in your hands like a newborn baby.
Transfixed by all the flashing colours 'click here', 'click here'.
Open 50,000 tabs at once because you might need them, maybe.
Tap until you crack my skin, overheat me till my insides fizz.

And when I die from overuse, I'll still store all your data.
Then you'll charge me back up so you can use me again later.

Audrey Robinson-Hall (14)
Banovallum School, Horncastle

Please Someone Help Me

There's no more time
This is a serious crime
All I can hear is the clock's deafening chime
I'm covered in my own grime.

No matter my circumstances I am still hopeful
Even though I'm feeling woeful
And my eyes shine in this dull light like opals
As I fulfil this total.

Please someone, help me
My death is a guarantee
As the floor collects the debris
All my heart desires is to flee.

My heart's racing faster than an F1 car
My heart is going to be scarred
Everyone seems to disregard
My body cracks like shards of glass.

Inside a silenced room I lay still
All I do is follow his will
Awaiting his kill
Trying to fulfil his thrill.

Please someone help me
My death is a guarantee

As the floor collects this debris
All my heart desires is to flee.

As he walks by I await the punishment
My face screams astonishment
When he's really a non-accomplishment.

I think of my escape plan whilst I act distraught
Hoping for support.
My fuse is becoming awfully short,
Waiting for a report.

Please someone help me,
My death is a guarantee.
As the floor collects this debris
All my heart desires is to flee.

I'm finally free, spreading my wings
Telling the people of his sins.
As people's brains enrage and spin
Knowing I will never trust anyone within.

Oliver Bushell (13)
Banovallum School, Horncastle

Misshapen By Society

I'm on the surface, at the top of a hill
I am unique and untouched, in my most natural form.
I need to get to the bottom of the hill to complete this complex journey
As I look down I see other rocks,
Not like me, so smart, so smooth, so rounded,
Do I need to be like them?
Somebody comes along and kicks me.
I start rolling down.
My bumps start to chip off,
I know this is not me, but if I want to beautiful, I have to keep rolling on
To become like the sparkly, shiny rocks people want me to be.

Oh, to become a diamond, valued and loved,
The diamond is somewhere in me,
I've just not found it yet.
I guess I'll keep rolling down to look like the other rocks.
Part of me is becoming dust, never to be seen again,
All over the place.
I have reached the end of the hill
I am nothing but dust.
Where was the diamond?
I have lost my sparkle that was in my bumps,
Becoming like them has not made me beautiful.

I wanted to be like them but I never was.
I was imperfect but beautiful.

Summer Shiel (13)
Banovallum School, Horncastle

The Frankfurt

I'm happy, excited
What's out there, I'm not sure
I'm in the jar watching everyone, everything.

Yes! I got picked
In the basket I am
Turning, twisting, rolling
I am out.

Cars, trees, life, but no air yet
I am still stuck
Will I be forever?

I am locked, no light
Every now and then I see a hand
It never picks me.

Four weeks it chose me
The lid is open
Air
It's great.

Something sharp stabbed me
It hurt but it pulled me out.

Splash!
Burn, pain, noise
It hurt, really hurts.

Finally, the pain is over
In a bun,
In a warm toasty it's great.

Half my body gone
The pain is back
Now only my head
I am gone
Gone.

Jessie Pearson (15)
Banovallum School, Horncastle

A New Hope

The breeze flows through the branches,
Leaves lightly fall to the yellowing grass.
Change lingers in the wind,
A new season is upon us,
From green to orange to red.
The melody of a summer day to the sound of an autumn tune.
With new seasons, a new year appears.
The winter approaches.
All the orange and red leaves have fallen and clings to the ground defensively.
The branches stand bare.
A new hope has reached, it's almost spring.
Though will the branches win?
Will they survive the fury of winter
The calming of the storm has neared
The hope is here
A new season has sprung
The branches grow small leaves once more
A light peeps through the branches of leaves
Spring is here, nothing to fear.

Daisy-May Simpson (12)
Banovallum School, Horncastle

On The Run

M ad high-speed chases send fear into victims and police alike,
U nknown to the unconscious victim they are in a high-speed chase,
R eddening walls of a van from past victims stain the walls,
D read-filled police chase the runaway killer and victim,
E erie silence fills the air as the terrifying chase continues,
R eady to ram the car the police close in.

V an's wheels screech when the car hits but the van continues,
I n the van, the murderer speeds up to make a getaway,
C ountless times the victim struggles to be free,
T he murderer loses the police after causing a crash,
I n the van the victim freaks,
M urderer only laughs as they get to kill again.

Evie Ladlow (13)
Banovallum School, Horncastle

Practising Recognition

The sun we lay under, shows no mercy for some
The Somalian heat burns through their will to continue
Sudden circumstances beyond control, forced these young souls to roam

To share the story of a young child caught up in the crossfire and chaos of war
Is to inspire, to build a world where no child knows of the fire.

To embrace the displaced, and empathise as if we are looking through their eyes.
To replace the turmoil they endure and restore peace and purity for them once more.

The hands and lungs of a child, worn down from exhaustion
This is how they are dying, dying to survive

Peace starts within, a choice we make
To let go of anger, for compassion's sake.

Tabitha Cameron (15)
Banovallum School, Horncastle

The Life Within

I woke as a small ember,
Soon to grow into a mysterious fire,
I crackled calmly, not watching the life around me,
Like the life I longed for.
As the wind howled, the night came,
It swept my flames with it.
My colours glowed within
As I grew into a monstrous inferno,
Consuming the life around me.
Snap. Crackle. Pop.
The wind died down, taking it with me.
I became an ember again.
All around me I heard nothing but saw ash and stone.
I longed for a life but my longing vanished,
I realised the life I longed for was here all along,
Within me all the time.
One last gust of wind and I had gone.

Eva Raimondo (11)
Banovallum School, Horncastle

Life In Hiding

The minute I was going to shut my eyes to fall asleep,
I could hear booming of the bombs dropped by the Allies,
I could hear Margot's shriek that rattled the walls of the hiding place as she read the letter from the Nazis.
I walked to the window,
Looked outside and I can remember the sight I saw.
I saw someone being shot by the Gestapo.
My heart skipped a beat as I realised if Margot didn't report to the train station
that would be her fate.
My heart sunk to my stomach and my eyes also began to tear up as my knees dropped to the ground.
I began to cry hysterically and the only thing to bring me comfort was my diary.

Libby Harness (12)
Banovallum School, Horncastle

Things Change Over Time

A seed in the soil of the earth that grows,
Change is inevitable and everyone knows,
The buzz of the bees in the warm summer air,
Winter that harbours the hibernating bear,
Life brought into the world in spring,
The brown leaves that autumn brings,
Change is inevitable and everyone knows.

Glaciers melting left and right,
Volcanic ash clouding the blue sky,
Mountains crumbling,
The Earth is tumbling,
Change is inevitable and everyone knows,
It is sometimes good and sometimes bad,
It reminds us of the little time we had.

Change is inevitable and everyone knows.

Caitlin Barnes (14)
Banovallum School, Horncastle

Trapped Before Release

A prison made by the boy's own making
Made with the chains by the boy's poor choices and twisted allure.
His eyes, like polished mirrors to the soul,
And have been grazed and tarnished by sin.
Though for a second, a glimmer of light
And a drop of soap being able to pierce even the toughest of his locks.
With the room flooding with negative thoughts,
The boy yearns for freedom against his dark choices and sadness.
And once the eyes seemed polished and clean,
Out came a changed kid,
Going to make things right once more.

Dylan Hillier (15)
Banovallum School, Horncastle

Diana's Reality

Good things aren't always what they seem,
But my children were the greatest things.
Good things aren't always what they seem,
My husband and his family took advantage of me.
Good things aren't always what they seem,
It felt like nobody was there for me.
Good things aren't always what they seem,
It felt like nobody even cared for me.
Good things aren't always what they seem,
My marriage was destroying me.
Bad things aren't always what they seem,
My marriage was over, was it the best for me?

Mariama Egan (15)
Banovallum School, Horncastle

Mrs Cow

The poor old cow watches the trees
Swaying in the wind, feeling the breeze,
A tear falls from his eye,
It runs down his cheek.
Wondering why he couldn't just die
Or at least see a peek of his future.
One day, just like the rest,
His world was put in the past
As he watched another cow walk towards him.
The poor old cow was no longer poor,
No longer old.
The cow is now torn between the grass and her.
The cow was no longer feeling old,
Doing as he's told from his new Mrs Cow.

Coen Warren (15)
Banovallum School, Horncastle

A Bin

They are a bin, they yearn for trash
But when you drop yours to the ground with a crash,
It's just out of their reach, and they yearn for more.
"Just feed it to me, it isn't a chore!
My food is extremely poisonous to other creatures!
For them it is not delicious!
If animals eat my trash they'll become deceased
So put that trash in the bin and let me feast!"
If you have any old food in the back of the fridge,
Give it to the bin not a landfill ditch!

Henry Williams (12)
Banovallum School, Horncastle

All Hope Is Not Lost

Waking up in a cold, dark place
Forced to work the entire day
Raised to be faithful, but then to be sold
Given away until they are old
Criticised for their own skin colour
Unfed, uncared for like no other
Given a chance, but it's gone like it came
Feel kind of hopeful but it's never the same
But one day, their suffering will go
Saying hello to the life they now know
A hero will come but not at a cost
Slaves are reassured that all hope is not lost.

Priya Bennett (12)
Banovallum School, Horncastle

The Humble Pen

Dead is how I felt when my ink ran out.
Betrayal is what coursed through me when I saw them use someone new.
Sadness is what overcame me when I realised I could not write words again.
Anger flooded my plastic body as everything went black.
I was in the depths of despair when everything came rushing to me when I realised I had been thrown away.
Surrounding my numb body I saw others like me.
Dead. Betrayal. Sadness. Despair.
Are all the emotions I felt when I died that day.

Ellie Burge (14)
Banovallum School, Horncastle

Sea Creatures

S eeing all the creatures gather the
E normous turquoise-like turtles
A ppear and the whale's voice hums near.

C rashing waves are now here
R apidly raving away
E ach creature now rushes home
A nd fish now under the stones.
T omorrow is hopefully better, as we will all be
U nited again. Dancing and swimming away
R eady for the next day and now only
E xcitement appears.

Bella Webster (12)
Banovallum School, Horncastle

War Diary

A war started
N o one was safe
N o one had everything they needed any more
E very Jew was in danger.

F inally, we were found
R ound they went
A nnihilating us all
N o one was safe
K icking us out of our homes
S tarting the horror.

D ying
I njuring
A lone
R eady to pass on
Y esterday is over and today never began for me.

Amelia Hennessy (12)
Banovallum School, Horncastle

Mental Health

M en's mental health matters
E veryone has problems
N ot everyone is very open about their mental health
T herapies are good, there are people who can help you
A lways there for you
L et people help you

H uman, experience this daily
E veryone can have help if needed
A wareness of anxiety
L earning coping skills
T herapy to help you
H ealthy minds.

Evie Booth (14)
Banovallum School, Horncastle

My Fate

Click! Flash! Click!
It all happens too quick
Never alone
Not even at home
Always in fear
Because people are near.
Cameras flash, voices rise
A mob of fans with staring eyes
All expecting something great
After all, it is my fate.
Always in the spotlight
And it is so bright
I wish I could step out
And live a normal life
But I cannot
So I guess I'll be okay
After all, it is my fate.

Skye Bown (14)
Banovallum School, Horncastle

Sweetheart

I'm here for her like she is for me
Running around next to her
Lying in her lap
All for comfort within her.
I bring happiness even in dark places
To fulfil the love within one person
To help with overwhelming emotions
To bring out happiness even in bright places.
I show comfort and confidence
To entertain and bring fun
To love and enjoy your presence
I shall not leave.

Megan Patnell
Banovallum School, Horncastle

You Are Not Alone

I miss my country but I'm also happy to leave.
I miss all my friends but I'm also happy to make new friends.
I miss my family but I'm also happy with my new one.
I miss my house but I'm also happy with my new one.

In the end, when life leaves you in the dark
Look in the light and things will get better.
You are not alone and you will always have someone to talk to.

Madeline Yates (12)
Banovallum School, Horncastle

Flying Over Blitz

Soaring through the skies
I don't know where I am
I don't know where I was
But all I know is that I have to help Great Britain's cause.

Soaring through the skies
I see the houses destroyed
I still remember the hopeful day
When I was first deployed.

Soaring through the skies
My metal skin so weak
Ash, scraps and sulphur
Makes me truly reek.

Arran Giffen (13)
Banovallum School, Horncastle

Pink Wild Fox

W ishing to see what the real world looks like
I n the dark, all alone, suddenly she turns to foam
L ike a raspberry, she turns bright pink
D evastated of her colour, she turns duller.

F rightened still, but trying her best.
O range she turns and suddenly, is happier.
X ylophone's running through the forest to celebrate her confidence.

Lily-Mai Garner-Jones (12) & Kiara Ross (12)
Banovallum School, Horncastle

Dreams

Football is like a dream
Some dreams don't always come true
Dreams are important
Because they are what you think about before
you fall asleep
Some dreams come true
But not all dreams last.
Dreams come and go as you grow
Dreams are important because at the end of the day,
dreams are what are important to you
Dreams don't always last but some do.

Paige Harrison (13)
Banovallum School, Horncastle

Wonders Of Football

The wonders of football are not always how they seem.
The wonders of football are not always a smooth stream.
The wonders of football are mostly a dream.
The wonders of football are almost never true.
Is my dream the wonder of football, or is it just reality?
The wonder of football comes and goes.
But what is the wonder of football?

Olivia Midgley (14)
Banovallum School, Horncastle

A Teacher's Day

T eaches you no matter the circumstances
E very day they give you their wisdom
A lways wanting to get the best out of you
C hallenging you until your limit
H ere to teach, never forget
E ven through the hardest times
R ead, write, achieve, that's what they give you in this life.

Jake Steele (12)
Banovallum School, Horncastle

Modelling Clay

Some wonder the difference
Between me and the normal stuff.
They use me to model
I am the artist's favourite.
People wonder how I'm made
People question where I'm from.
My texture is rough but can be made smooth
People make expensive things out of me.
You put me in a kiln
I am modelling clay.

Liam Jones
Banovallum School, Horncastle

The Life Of A Soldier

As a trembling teen he goes to Iraq and risks his life
Welcomed home with a medal
And off he goes again, missing Christmas this time.
This time welcomed home with three hugs
Summer hits, he is relaxing in the garden
Dad, Dad, someone's calling
With tears in his eyes, he packs his bags and off he goes again.

Toby Rawdon (12)
Banovallum School, Horncastle

The Refugee

Cold, dark and bleak,
This is what they live in.
They go through this every day.
They live in the dark with no light.
We need to help them find a home.
They all hope that one day they will find a home.
They are hoping that one day light will shine through again.
This is what it is like for a refugee.

Harriet Gleeson (12)
Banovallum School, Horncastle

That King

One day, not long ago,
A king sat upon his throne,
He was pondering an old query,
"Does anyone like me?"
With the sheer amount of Republicans
And this king isn't a magician
He couldn't make them like him,
Not even writing it in solid pen,
Wait, that doesn't rhyme!

George Hickling (12)
Banovallum School, Horncastle

The Bomb

I am massive destruction
I am hell above
My bomb bay doors open
You watch me fall
My mushroom cloud rises
I am seen before I am heard
I will destroy
The people evaporate
There is mist left
The people are nonexistent
Radiation crosses along the land
I am the bomb.

Archie Fincham
Banovallum School, Horncastle

The Neglected Book

I sit on a shelf
By myself
Day and night,
Hoping for life.
Collecting years of dust
You've never picked me up.
It takes five minutes a day to read a page
But no, you don't
You spend your day playing your game.
As I lie there unread...
Dusty...
Forgotten.

Faith Fenwick (15)
Banovallum School, Horncastle

Tooth Vs Human

D ecaying tooth I am
E namel is eroding away
N o matter what I do I can't lose the pain
T ime is ticking before I go to sleep
I ncisors soon become rotten
S lowly the teeth will fall
T ime soon passes and the dentist will call.

Alice Skayman (13)
Banovallum School, Horncastle

Disguised Fame

Day after day
Person after person
Endless attention
Unnecessary attention
Sometimes I like it
Sometimes I don't
Sometimes I want to be alone
Sometimes I want the people
Hundreds of people
But I will always like my life.

Leah Walls (15)
Banovallum School, Horncastle

What Am I?

At the start I'm small and delicate
Then I start to grow
Cold and frozen
Till the winter goes.
As the temperature rises
The sun begins to glow
You start to have some fun
Until you see the mow.

What am I?

Noah Sim (12)
Banovallum School, Horncastle

Criminal Is Bad!

C riminal is bad
R aining with blood
I llegal to kill people
M oney robber
I ntruder is here
N ow is the time for killing
A killer walks in
L aw-breaker.

Bella Evans (13)
Banovallum School, Horncastle

Echoes Of The Battlefield

In the stillness of night, my mind returns,
To fields of battle where the memory burns.
A soldier's path, through mud and blood,
In the echo of silence, the haunting flood.
I am but a ghost of the man I used to be,
Lost in the fog, where no one can see.
Faces of comrades lost in the fray,
Visit my dreams, never fading away.
The roar of guns, the cries of pain,
Tattooed on my soul, a permanent stain.
I carry the weight of the lives we've lost,
A burden so heavy it came at a cost.
By day, I walk through a world so changed,
Yet inside my mind, the scenes are unchanged.
I smile, I nod, I try to blend in,
But inside the chaos, wars still begin.
How do I tell them of the nights I weep,
Of shadows that invade the realm of sleep?
In the daylight's glare, they see me whole,
But they don't know the cracks within my soul.
Every loud noise makes my heart race,
In every stranger's glance, an enemy's face.
I yearn for peace, a quiet mind,
To leave the horrors far behind.

Lovepreet Singh (14)
Grove Academy, Slough

Reminisce

In the quiet stillness, the wind softly sings,
Of a winter storm lost in unseen wings.
Beneath my feet, the snow lies cold and pale,
As memories linger, leaving a haunting trail.

The town stands empty, a ghostly sight,
Evacuated, swallowed by the night.
I struggle to move, burdened by the past,
Trapped in a moment that couldn't last.

Each step through the snow, a heavy weight.
Dragging me down, sealing my fate.
Stains of blood, footprints in the snow,
Tell a story of loss, of letting go.

I long for a different ending, a brighter day,
But the cold reality won't fade away.
The air is thick with unspoken words,
Echoing the silence, like distant birds.

Whispers of winter carried on the breeze,
A tale of sorrow, of shattered ease.
In the stillness of the empty town,
I find solace in the snow, falling down

Well, that's that, then.
Can't do anything about it, right?

Not sure what the takeaway there is from this...
...if there even is anything to learn.

I steadily move away...
My hoodie gently tugged back against the movements.
A faint familiar smile graces my shoulders...
But that's probably just my imagination.

Ahmed Tarar (14)
Grove Academy, Slough

Embracing Your Emotions

In the heart's silent chambers, emotions reside,
A spectrum of feelings we often let hide.
From sorrow's deep shadows to joy's radiant light,
Embrace every whisper, each day and each night.
Let anger's fierce tempest roar wild and free,
Then calm it with patience, like waves on the sea.
Love with abandon, let kindness flow wide,
In the embrace of these feelings, your true self abide.
Joy lifts your spirit, like wings on the breeze,
Sadness brings wisdom, puts the heart at ease.
In the dance of emotions, let your soul find its voice,
For in embracing each feeling, you honour, your choice.
So cherish each moment, let your heart lead the way,
In the storm and the sunshine, in the night and the day.
Through the embrace of emotions, your spirit will grow,
For they are the compass that helps you to know.

Leonie Ward (15)
Grove Academy, Slough

You Are Not Alone

Life gets harder day by day,
No time to think, no time to play.
When you are feeling a lot of stress,
It is best to confess.

When you are feeling down,
Just know that there are people around.
If you are overthinking please don't,
You should know you are not alone.

Be grateful for all you had,
Please don't ever get mad or sad.
Think about the positive, not what puts you down,
Never ever let yourself drown.

Life is full of opportunities,
Doesn't matter in which community.
Dont mind the people who always have something to say,
Everyone looks their own way.

Lara Costa (14)
Grove Academy, Slough

Through Their Eyes

Through their eyes,
A butterfly flies.
Through their eyes
Oh, what goes on in their mind?
To be so blind
What could you find
Through their eyes,
A butterfly flies.
As fragile as can be
At least that's what we see.

Through their eyes,
A mirror smiles.
Deep inside their face
Which goes on for miles.
Their mind is so fragile
Losing a mental battle
Through their eyes,
A mirror smiles.

A single mean word
Hurt as much as spikes
To their mind,
It's as scary as a dark night.
Through their eyes,
All alone,

They're frozen,
Frozen to the bone.

Through their eyes,
A helping hand
Stretches far,
Like a rubber band.
Through their eyes,
You're not alone
There is just more than there is shown.

Ashley S (12)
Grove Academy, Slough

Is This How I Truly Feel?

Outside we are meant to feel free
But why do I disagree?
I feel enclosed even with those around me
Even with friends
My teeth clench.
Clench like a clamshell

I'm silent, with no words
My leg follows them like a herd
I'm silent, with no words

At least the clouds can relate
Floating together
But even they can make bad weather
It cries like most
The wind cries like a ghost

Outside we are meant to feel happy
Yet I feel no privacy
Is this how I truly feel?
As I say in therapy.

Aurora Sahiti (15)
Grove Academy, Slough

Mental Health

M ake every day count,
E ngage in activities you love,
N ever give up,
T ake care of yourself,
A ppreciate the good times you spent with your friends and family,
L isten to others who need your help,

H ave some fun with your friends and family to reduce stress,
E very person has, or had, a difficult day,
A lways try your best,
L earning new things makes your mind clearer and more relaxed,
T ake care of your health,
H ave some fresh air.

Kacper Kowalenko (15)
Grove Academy, Slough

You Are Not Alone

Darkness binder, sometimes a secret keeper
Going through inner battles and a midnight weeper
Hopes faintly glimmer during a dawn light bringer
The healings whisper and a heartstring singer

Everyone makes mistakes, it's a part of life
If not him or her, it's someone living
Don't stay stressed rather be relaxed
See the change it will cause no pain

Everyone has ups and downs
Sometimes brave, sometimes not
Life can get tough so don't make it worse
So think twice and be wise!

Vanessa Pereira (14)
Grove Academy, Slough

Is It Enough?

When everything is going wrong
And you are struggling to carry on
But you still smile and help
I want you to remember
Is it enough?

When you are feeling the hurt and pain
And try your hardest to stay sane
The problems climbing to your head
Like the snakes climbing a tree

When you feel you've no one to care
Remember there is someone there
I want you to know you matter.

Cristian Georgescu (15)
Grove Academy, Slough

Drunk In Love

You met in school,
Known each other since babies,
One day you asked her to be your lady,
On the phone night and day,
But you never ask her if she's okay.

She hates the way you make her laugh,
But even worse when you make her cry,
She texts you now and then,
But you don't love her like you did then,
It's now been two long years,
But she is still drunk in love.

Natalia Brodowicz (13)
Grove Academy, Slough

Be Positive

Listen for the positive
The voice that talks you down
The one that tells you that they care
Make sure to play it fair

And when you're standing on the ledge
Don't think you're gonna fall off the edge
They're waiting in the wings
Make sure it's not a breeze of wind
Remember that life is full of hope and other things

Stay positive.

Princess Chantelle Zivurawa (14)
Grove Academy, Slough

In The Whispers Of The Mind

In the whispers of the mind, storms gently brew,
Fears and worries dance, wearing shades of blue.
Mental health is a fragile bloom to tend with care,
Embracing imperfections, finding strength to bear.

In the chaos of thoughts, we seek a light,
To guide us through the darkest night.
With courage and strength, we face the day,
Knowing it's okay to not be okay.

Floria Sony (15)
Grove Academy, Slough

My Inner Darkness

In the trenches, darkness swells,
My mind's a storm, where silence dwells.
Bombs explode, I can't escape
Memories haunt, they don't take breaks.

Shadows whisper, ghosts of friends,
Sleepless nights, that never end,
Just a kid, but I've grown old,
My heart feels heavy, stories untold.

Szymonek C (14)
Grove Academy, Slough

Nuclear War

In the eerie glow of nuclear dawn,
Where life once thrived, now ghosts are drawn,
Silent echoes of a world once grand,
Now ashes and cinders, a desolated land.
Humanity's folly, a fatal spark,
Lighting the way through the cold and dark,
In the pursuit of power.

Koshin Aweys (13)
Grove Academy, Slough

Endangered Species

The years pass by
Suffering from plastic inside
The animals start to die
Nor can live
Nor can die
The screaming, suffering can't be heard
Can't do a thing, can't say a word
Animals and plants are dying outside,
So, what are we doing inside?

Sanjana Sree Rajaram (14)
Grove Academy, Slough

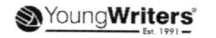

It's Okay Not To Be Okay

Anxiety is normal
So don't think you're abnormal
Life can get tough
So don't make it worse

Don't keep things in your heart
Just know you don't have to look apart
Don't listen to people who talk bad
It's okay to get sad.

Betjina Rebelo (14)
Grove Academy, Slough

Tides Of The Mind

A diamanté poem

Chaos,
Stormy, turbulent
Falling, spiralling, drowning
Anxiety, fear, confusion, darkness
Whispers, calm, clarity
Rising, shining, soaring
Peaceful, tranquil
Serenity.

Elvis Nkongo (14)
Grove Academy, Slough

Far From Home

Far from home
Nowhere to go
All alone in this world
That's cold
I don't want to be alone
With no one to hold
I want to go home
Where I won't be alone.

Moroyinmola Ogundimu (13) & Bihter
Grove Academy, Slough

Just Accept Me, Darling

I am your sunshine,
I am your wind,
I am your water,
Oh, what do I do
Oh, what do I do
For you to accept me?

Ibrahim Ahmer (12)
Grove Academy, Slough

Eternal Companion; Ode To Friendship

In the dance of life, a constant beat,
A melody played by two hearts sweet.
Through the ebb and flow of time's swift tide,
Stands a friend, forever by my side.
In laughter shared beneath the azure sky,
Or tears we shed when sorrows fly,
Hand in hand, we weather every storm,
In your embrace, I find my calm.
Like the oak that stands against the gale,
You're my rock when doubts assail.
In your eyes, I see a mirror true,
Reflecting all I am, and all of you.
In whispers shared beneath the moon's soft glow,
Or secrets kept that only we know,
Our bond is forged by trust's golden thread,
A treasure trove where words need not be said.
Through the seasons, our friendship blooms,
Like a flower in the garden's looms.
In your laughter, I find my joy,
My dearest friend, my soul's envoy.
So here's to you, my cherished mate,
In this journey, let's navigate.
Hand in hand, we'll brave the bend,
Forevermore, my faithful friend.

Japji Kaur
King Edward VI Handsworth School For Girls, Handsworth

Carlos Sainz 55

Carlos Sainz, a racing star,
With speed and skill, he goes far.
On the track, he takes command,
A true master of the racing land.

With every turn, he dances and glides,
His car, a beast, as it swiftly rides.
Through the corners, he finds his groove,
Leaving his rivals in the dust to prove.

His determination, fierce and strong,
He races with heart, all race long.
Fearless and bold, he takes the lead,
A champion's spirit, indeed.

Carlos Sainz, a name we cheer,
A legend in the racing sphere.
With every victory, he leaves his mark,
A true inspiration, lighting up the dark.

Eva Donoghue (14)
Maricourt Catholic High School, Liverpool

Opinions

In a world full of noise, opinions abound,
Everybody talking, but who's really profound?
Some lift you up, while others tear you down,
Don't let 'em get to you, stand your ground.

Opinions are like whispers in the wind,
Blowing left and right, always trying to bend,
Your truth, your path, don't let them offend,
Stay strong, stay true, your voice will transcend.

So speak your mind, be bold and bright,
Don't let others dim your light,
Opinions are many, but your future's in sight,
Rise above the chatter, own your fight.

What people say doesn't really matter
Because at the end of the day, it's just chatter
Against all odds, I'll always fight,
In the pursuit of my dreams, I'll never say goodbye.
Through the struggles and the tears,
I conquer doubts, shatter fears,
My goals that are within reach, crystal clear,
In the realm of dreams, I engineer.

No stopping now, keep pushing through,
My dreams are in focus, always in view,
With every step, my spirit grew,
In this game of dreams, I stay true.

So let the world doubt and scheme,
I'll keep moving forward, living my dream,
In this life, nothing's as it seems,
But I'll keep rising, in my dreams, supreme.

Zuha Irfan (13)
Maricourt Catholic High School, Liverpool

The Way My Mother Reminisces

In the twilight of childhood, my dear one strides,
A *teenager now*, with dreams that reach the skies.
From innocence to independence, you swiftly soar,
Leaving behind the days of toys scattered on the floor.

In your eyes, I glimpse the storm and the calm,
As you navigate the path, a beautiful balm.
With every step, you carve *your own* way,
Unfurling your wings to greet the break of day.

The days of bedtime tales and play,
Replaced by conversations that linger these days.
Yet in your laughter, I still hear the child within,
A melody of memories, where love has always been.

Through teenage angst and rebellious flare,
I stand beside you, always *present*, always *there*.
For in your journey of self-discovery and strife,
I offer my guidance, my wisdom, my life.

Oh, my teenage child, with a heart so bold,
In your stories untold, may your spirit unfold.
Embrace the challenges, the highs and lows,
For in every stumble, a seed of wisdom grows.

So spread your wings, my darling, and take flight,
With courage as your compass, and love as your light.

In the dance of adolescence, find your way,
Knowing *I'll be here*, come what may.

Hannah Robinson (15)
Maricourt Catholic High School, Liverpool

The Alarm Clock

All alone I sat
Staring at the empty bed
Waiting all alone
For my friend to rest her head
Then came a knocking
A knocking at the door
My friend had come to bed
To go to sleep once more
Sound asleep she was
As the sound of snoring could be heard
Eyes fluttering around
With not a single word
My time was ticking
Ticking sweet and soft
The only noise in the room
Just louder than a moth
Then when the time struck
Excitedly did I chime
Then angrily she turned her head
And let out a little whine
She was upset with me
And what I had done
When all I wanted to do
Was get her ready for a day of fun
She stared at me deadly
As she flung me to the floor

So I just waited there all day
For my time to chime once more.

Abbie Stokes (14)
Ponteland High School, Ponteland

I Am Death

I come in the night,
I come in the day,
Nothing you do will keep me away.

When day dawns,
Or night falls,
You're alone with no one to call.

I'll keep you company,
I'll be your friend,
But inevitably, I am your end.

I am there for you,
In a strange sort of way,
And I am NOT what they portray.

You don't understand,
My job is tough,
But all must end, soon enough.

You might be scared,
Just take my hand,
I'll bring you to the Fairyland.

I am Death,
You may have guessed,
But now, finally, you can rest.

Kate Massie (14)
Ponteland High School, Ponteland

The Little Things

Every day used as usual,
Not taken notice of,
Not valued how they should be,
The little things,
Never noticed.

The silk fluff comfort,
Sat down on every day,
The cross-stitching pattern along the back,
And the sturdy legs used to hold,
Never noticed.

The sweet chirping of birds outside,
Lighting up the awaking morning,
The sunrise opens up its arms,
To start the day strong,
Never noticed.

The old man you walk past every morning,
That smiles at you on the way,
Giving you that feeling inside,
That life is better than you think,
Never noticed.

Joseph Harrington (14)
Ponteland High School, Ponteland

The Sea Is Blue

Many are scared of my deep depths,
Scared of the creatures which lurk beneath.
Many are scared of the unknown,
Many are scared of *me*.

Many say I am unpredictable,
That I'm destructive and a harbour of bad news.
They believe that one wrong move and I'll drag them under,
All the way down to the ocean floor.

I am violent,
I am merciless,
I am tempestuous,
Yet, I am never truly *me*.

Skye Rutherford (13)
Ponteland High School, Ponteland

The Importance Of Life

Once you are there, don't be in despair;
Those who are penurious will not care.
The wise words of those who have lived it
Are now far away from there.
The importance of life.
Only 9 decades, some are lucky others, seldom.
No one can inform only you once you're born
Life is full of memories; those you have lost,
Things you have done make granted in life
As opportunities only pop up once.

Miles Lunn (14)
Ponteland High School, Ponteland

The Search

I hike mountains,
And ride the sea.
I travel roads,
And the places you don't see.

I fly high,
And drop low.
I take lefts,
When there are rights no more.

I move forwards,
I move backwards,
I do turns all around.
Searching for a home,
A home nowhere to be found.

Ibrahim Choudhary (14)
Ponteland High School, Ponteland

The Pet's Eyes

When I look at you I see,
Warmth and happiness,
You remind me
Of my very own mother back home,
When you come through the front door,
Joy fills my heart,
My tail beats off the floor,
Imagine you are tired and fed up,
I'll cheer you up.

Will Alderson (13)
Ponteland High School, Ponteland

Through The Eyes Of A Floor

I hate it when people tread on my face
It hurts like a thousand bees stinging me
Or even like a bullet shot to my head,
Especially when they stamp their feet
When they get angry over little things
Plus when they put loads of furniture on me
The weight is like holding the sky up
It's as painful as being crushed by a whole building
Hm, ironic I hold up those things, that aches too.
Why must they do this to me?
I'm just an innocent floor that's done nothing.
Or that monster called the vacuum cleaner.
He ruins my day, rubbing his fluff all over me,
Cleaning up my crumbs. Sure, I like that.
But he is smooshing his face against me, it hurts
And the noise... Is he mad?
He's gotta have so much ignorance to do that.

And now my least favourite things...
Heels. I. Hate. Heels. Like really?
Why must you smash your stupid spikes into me?
It's painful. A shoe with basically a dagger and a flat part?
It's horrendous! I honestly just don't get it.
Ugh... Anyway, time for some good things.

I like it when children walk on me.
It's so nice and light... almost like a cloud,

Gliding across the floor, it's beautiful
I love it. There is nothing bad about those kids
Wow, nothing better than when people treat me well.
It's so nice and such a kind act.

And the mind to cover me with a carpet? Wow.
I. Hold. Your. Buildings. Up. For. You.
The ignorance, oh, the ignorance...
I do so much for you.
Yet you treat me like nothing.
Anyway, I'll stop ranting now. Have a good day!

Joseph Pringle (12)
Reddam House Berkshire, Wokingham

Through The Eyes Of My Dog, Waffle

How she reveres at my glorious sight,
As I wag my tail, with all my might
My big brown eyes, dilate its pupils
As they glint near the table light

My feet, always padding along your side,
Either on wood, marble or grass,
The only noise to always miss,
That you would keep close to your heart.

I plead for food, at the kitchen counter,
But kibble for dogs?
We deserve a quite grander feast,
Therefore be careful.
We are heedful of your every move
As you eat all your food.

As we munch on happy grass,
We bask in the sun,
It's quite a blast!
Running around,
Playing with toys, being silly.

But what I find so mysterious is,
How humans stare at a screen,
The more I look the more I'm keen
For them to watch their screen

From cricket to comedy shows,
It's interesting to see what these humans watch next

My favourite activity of all,
Staring at those people on their walk.
Barking at them to leave as I put my paws up
On the white windowsill,
Wagging my tail as I continue this din of barks,
For those humans should never lark too close to my house.

When my favourite humans leave
My tail, myself, stays quiescent
As my tail curls into a question mark.
As I wonder why you leave
Oh, my sadness you can see.

Most parts of my day
I check on these humans
To see what they're doing.
Nothing interesting?
Well then, let's take a nap
It never gets boring.

Saanvi Sharma (12)
Reddam House Berkshire, Wokingham

Through The Eyes Of My Cat

I clamber the rooftops,
Jumping from fence to fence.
I run vigorously,
Trying to catch up to pigeons.
They always slip from my clutches,
Dancing in the moonlit ribbons.

I sleep on the sofa,
Dropping my defence.
I steal my owner's seats,
But she doesn't mind.
She loves me,
And I love her back.

I defend my territory,
Standing proud and strong.
I don't let anyone enter,
Or stick around for too long.

I have watched my owner's children grow up,
And encouraged them all the way.
I comforted them when they hurt themselves,
And it made the pain go away.

When I feel sleepy,
I curl up into a ball.
I put myself in a place that smells like family,
And stay there all day long.

I don't mind if the children bother me,
They don't mean any harm.
They're just trying to say I love you,
That I've been there for them,
All the way along.

There has been an abundance of times,
That I have felt alone.
But whenever I feel like this,
I look into the caring faces,
And they say
"Don't worry, no!"

Through all of this,
There's something beneath my bravado.
It's something niggling, something big,
It's the feeling I get when I remember
That I have a place I can call home.

Zoe Macbeth (11)
Reddam House Berkshire, Wokingham

Through The Eyes Of A Sick, Dying Man

It has been a year since I fell
The time has come to bid farewell
Time was cut short by the result
My sons, don't think it was your fault

Who knew this disease would kill me fast
At least you are safe at last
Don't worry about the chemical's effect no more
The factory finally closed its door
So it is time that I do the same
Goodbye, my sons, may we meet again
Goodbye, my love, we've had fun
But now my friends I am done

Barely conscious now, fading in and out
While I write my final words to you
I love you without a doubt.
My eyes flicker through this letter and shed tears too

Friends and other dear relatives
We all had our future dreams
Mine is now sealed for eternity
Thank you for our last drink
I am on the brink

Stay strong
Stay lively

Live long
And thrive

Good luck in your future careers
Good luck taking your shares

Finally, goodbye, for my time is done
It is now time that I move on...

Hongyi Hu (11)
Reddam House Berkshire, Wokingham

Through The Eyes Of Poseidon

All my fish are dying
It's all these stupid mortals
They keep polluting my sacred waters
And nobody was stopping them
I had to send tidal waves for respect
Even then I was thought to be a myth

Zeus is so big-headed
The rest of the gods follow his lead
I am way better in more ways than one
He has a bolt and I have a trident
I lead with love he leads with fear

I was made to take an oath to have no more kids
Even worse Zeus broke that oath
No one blamed him but the Styx
Hades never broke the oath and surprised us all
Everyone blamed me and I came off worst

The Romans hated me
They feared me for their lives
The praetors spread superstitions about me
They left my shrine to rot
I was never happy even though the Greeks loved my son

I am restrained to one child visit a year
Zeus gets unlimited visits each year
This hurts me and I want to disobey

I want Hades or myself to lead Olympus
Obviously, Zeus disagrees but I don't care.

Oliver Thompson (11)
Reddam House Berkshire, Wokingham

Through The Eyes Of A Witness

Watching a dispute of two friends
It feels like it will never end
Both want me on their side
I know they will both collide
Both have biased accounts
The pressure builds up, it's too much
I hear shouting voices in my ear
Which makes me want to disappear
As the noise goes through my ears
I want to burst into tears
Hatred and anger dance through the air
But I just want nothing more than not to care
This shouting aloud attracts a growing crowd
Everyone watches with their eyes open wide
But all I want to do is run inside
Everyone is screaming,
I know this argument will ignite
One lands a punch and jumps up in glee
The other gets up and pounds on a tree
The crowd piles up and it's hard to see
To my surprise, a teacher arrives
"Stop!" she shouts and separates the two
In shock, the two stop like an alarm clock
Now to my desire the fight has stopped.

Josh Jain (12)
Reddam House Berkshire, Wokingham

A Refugee In London

The waves crash, and so does my mind
With thoughts of London, what would I find?
I'm one of 100, on a half-sunken raft
Everyone giddy but with shattered hearts

As the boat hauls the rope, we all pile out
And what I am met with, I still think about
Where were the burkas, the boys selling naan?
The graffiti and posters about the Taliban?

Women were free, their faces on show
The buses roared past as they took people home
Food is plenty and sweet music plays
Surely this means Heaven's a place

But as I walk onward, I'm shocked to see
How much of their sheer luxury is thrown away
in front of me
I walk down a street and see a joyful boy
And to my surprise, he has countless lovely toys!

We're taken to our families
And as I walk through the door
A sigh showers over me
I've turned my back on the war.

Daniel Marston (11)
Reddam House Berkshire, Wokingham

Through The Eyes Of A Sofa

I hate those stinky bums,
Though I have to admit
I like those mums.

I hate the dads that sit on me,
Like I am a useless, lifeless thing.

I might be mad,
But what I know is,
I love those beautiful mums,
Whose bodies light up my miserable pungent life.

Can they not be the only ones,
Who come and sit on me,
Weighing the weight of a feather.
I feel like I am on air.

But then the dads come and rub their butt on me,
Leaving dents bigger than their bodies,
They weigh two of me,
I fear I might collapse into a lifeless soul.

Don't even get me started on the babies,
I still have the stain from that day,
The most treacherous day of my life,
When the baby vomited all over my lovely silk.

Why oh why,
Why was I the chosen one,

The comfiest sofa chosen to mankind.
Why?

Ahria Modi (11)
Reddam House Berkshire, Wokingham

Through The Eye Of A Minecraft Wolf

I see the eyes of my parents
Destruction embedded in my eyes
I lost them, like black losing white
This moment, I lost my burning heart
The one I loved had left me

A human saw me,
Or should I say a player?
He has the bone.
My beloved ones said,
Bones are needed for us.
He tamed me.

I was taken to his home.
It was an exotic one
Wood, stone, planks.
He took me exploring in places.
Meadows, forests and mushroom islands
We went back home.

The player left for the day.
I waited, 1 day, 10 days.
There were cobwebs running around,
It started raining on day 15
He. Never returned.
His house had decayed

I know that he won't return
Maybe school, or war.
But I will still stay here to wait
Even for eternity.

Andy Fang (11)
Reddam House Berkshire, Wokingham

Through The Eyes Of A River

I wish to say
How to sway
To the flow of me
And be free
The world shall see
What I will be
They pollute
When they commute
The water is green
But never clean
There is always murk
That looks like a smirk
I used to have fish
Now they are all on a dish
The eggs are not there
Never treated with care
The beavers have no trees
And they can't eat cheese
The dam is breaking
The wood is flaking
The otters are the same
And who are they to blame
If they leave
Then it means they don't believe
I am dying
No longer flying

If you are there
Then will you care?
To restore the world
That has been unfurled
If you will
Then I won't spill.

Benjamin Wand (12)
Reddam House Berkshire, Wokingham

The Inescapable Walls

My cell door swung open.
It bashed against the wall.
All the prisoners walked out of their cells half awake.
The food was horrible
And the outdoors could be compared to a dumpster.
It felt like it was just yesterday,
That I was roaming the streets freely
To being pinned down on the floor.
In a matter of seconds, everything changed.
From good to bad.
All in slow motion,
Publicly, I had been humiliated, disgraced
And shunned by everyone around me.
My life was changing for the worse.
Do you know how that takes a toll on you?
You have to experience it to know it.
The feeling of anxiety, stress.
The walls here are nothing like what I used to know.

Tobi Okanlawon (12)
Reddam House Berkshire, Wokingham

The Disappearing Light

As the door swings behind me, I'm swept up in her arms,
I curl right up into a ball, and snuggle in, disarmed,
But just as quickly, my ears turn prickly and hear the fridge door close,
I twist and turn and yowl and screech, escaping this pose,

I trot over to the kitchen and size up my opponent,
I think it'll open if I jump, getting caught up in the moment,
But just as I'm about to leap, a light catches my eye,
I watch it for a moment... before letting my paws fly,

I jump and roll and run around,
Looking like a clown,
And then finally I squash it,
But when I lift my paw up,
It's nowhere to be found.

Daniela Passov (12)
Reddam House Berkshire, Wokingham

Through The Eyes Of An Author

I create and I destroy
Magical worlds are my toy
Characters great and small
Emerge from the paper upon I scrawl
Pages filled, lines brimming
Word upon word I'm winning

Twists and turns
Cause your eyes to burn
Heart-breaking, eye-catching
Emotions toyed with
Deaths fortifying my wonderful creations

But though everything seemed so perfect
Every great story must end
Even my own story will end one day
I will flutter away finally free
My body no longer holding me down
But I know I will not be forgotten
As my creations will be passed down through time.

Owen Storrie (12)
Reddam House Berkshire, Wokingham

A Poem Of A Vegan

A person in front of me,
Eating the creatures of the sea,
Stay calm, don't look,
Just keep reading your book,
I am so disgusted,
As I adjusted my position, looking away,
You're like an animal eating its prey,
Go somewhere I am not,
The food would fit perfectly in the bin slot,
Don't they realise I am vegan,
I can't get that image out of my head,
I should have just said,
Now I am lying in bed,
Trying to get that scene out of my head.

Poppy White (11)
Reddam House Berkshire, Wokingham

Through The Eyes Of My Dead Mother's Ghost

My hand stretches out
As I stare in disbelief
Is this who I'm supposed to be?
Invisible, lost and forgotten

I glide down the alleyway
And I hear a distant noise
It's getting closer and closer
And filled with fright I hide

But then I remember
And I slowly emerge from the shadows
My eyes widened in shock
As I saw myself - alive.

Ritvika Anandhakrishnan (12)
Reddam House Berkshire, Wokingham

I Am Homeless

I wish I could tell you how hard it is being me, a person who sleeps on the cold streets wondering

A homeless person is who I am, I spend my days roaming the streets with no place to call home

M any people would judge me, but they do not know the battles I have fought

H oping that one day I would be like one of those people, in a mansion buying all the latest fashion

O ne little act of kindness can bring hope and repair my heart

M y dreams guide me through the night, shining ever so bright, leading me to where I should go and telling me why I should be

E very person deserves a place to call home, deserving of a place that is fair, deserving someone to call family

L ife has changed for me, from living in a home to a shelter and lastly on the cold street

E very day is a new place for me, a new challenge and difficulties will help me rise

S treets have now become my shelter, cold and dark, starving for a glimmer of light and spark

S ick and tired of my life, not having enough money to afford a place to sleep. I just want a home.

Diya Odedra (12)
Rushey Mead Academy, Leicester

How I See The World

Through tear-filled eyes, my world unfolds
Once vibrant green, now etched with scars of old.
The thundering boom, a progress bold
Left skies choked grey, a story yet untold.

In the beginning, mankind was evolving,
Then boom! We had the industrial revolution
Which today, is still the cause of the world's pollution
The world was crying for a solution.

Greenhouse gases emitted from gas-guzzling machines on the roads
Air pollution caused by planes flying high in the skies.
To re-use, recycle and reduce we were told
Single-use plastics were no longer being sold
Was this enough?

Things only got worse as Earth sobbed sorrowfully
In a fit of rage, forest fires spread wildly
Earthquakes shattered the ground beneath us
But did we pay heed, or did we just take it all too mildly?

Our water is tainted with lead
Our crops grown with chemicals
Our air filled with toxins
Our future generation...
Our world.

Climate change impacts us all
Whether wealthy or in poverty
Today, the coast of Pakistan or Florida US
Tomorrow, a city near you.

Can we change the world?
We can certainly try for our and future generation
Together, we can be the change.

This world we share, in our entrusted hands
Let's rewrite fate, across the ravaged lands.

Zara Jamal (13)
Rushey Mead Academy, Leicester

Take Action For Our Wonderful World

The world is changing, can't you see?
Technology taking over, video games are key
Board games forgotten, family time lost
Gaming all day, at what cost?

Our lives are evolving, global warming near
Jobs shifting, be kind, have no fear
We're all unique, special in our own way
Let's celebrate differences, make each day a new display

Less talk, more action, let's unite
Fight together, make the future bright
Switch off devices, see the real world
Appreciate its beauty, let your flag unfurl

Take a moment, breathe it all in
This wonderful world, let's begin
To make a difference, together we stand
Hand in hand, let's lend a helping hand

So let's come together, make a change
Celebrate our differences, rearrange
Less hate, more love, let's spread joy

Let's take action now, together as one
For a better future, let's get it done
So switch off, step out, and see
The beauty of this world, let's set it free

To show everyone what we can really be
Let's make a difference, you and me
With love and kindness, let's make it right
Together, we can shine so bright.

Kecy Jignesh (12)
Rushey Mead Academy, Leicester

Through The Eyes Of A Mother

I wake up at the crack of dawn to see your precious smile,
I get out of bed and sit in solitude for a while.
I start to think about the moon and the stars,
Which planet I'll end up on, maybe Earth, maybe Mars.

You walk into the room, wondering which cereal to take,
Or maybe if you want the special pancakes that I make!
But wait, I forget, you're not 'my baby boy' anymore,
"I'm sorry I forgot!" but then you slammed the door.

At home, I do all the chores and work for you,
I even attempted to make your favourite 'fast food'.
After hours of tireless work and isolation,
I lie down but, in my chest, I feel a magical sensation.

I brush it away and open the door to let you in,
You said school was boring and chucked my food in the bin.
I hold back tears whilst trying to stay awake,
But sometimes it's too hard for me to fake.

Darkness precedes me for the rest of eternity,
But maybe I'll pop around as a ghost or entity.
I send you love and prayers from your mum,
Remember me forever as you will forever be my son...

Jai Kukadia (12)
Rushey Mead Academy, Leicester

Fields Of Friendship

Through their eyes, I see a field
A field with one dandelion in the distance
She picked it up in an instant
She said, "I wish to find a friend in this field."
She was so sure that her wish would come true
So then, she blew
The pollen went up and flew away
Then came the next day...

Through their eyes, I see the sunlight was teasing through the trees
And the bees could be heard amongst the gentle breeze
Near the meadow, in the field, I see a little girl no longer alone
There was now another, she seemed a clone
The two looked alike and started to dance into the night
The moon was so bright
It was such a beautiful sight

Through their eyes, I see a promise being made
They are whispering that they will be friends forevermore
They will never be alone again
Through their eyes.

Yashvi Chauhan
Rushey Mead Academy, Leicester

Owl's Riverscape

I scanned the moments of my life.
I floated across the seas,
I crawled through moorland,
Full of freedom was my time.

Hunting for food all night,
Sick, weary, drained, was I.
Tears falling all night,
End of aspiration, was I.

Blue cloudy sky had taken control,
In the night.
Pink cloudy crystals had disappeared,
Into the light.

Unaware of the surroundings was I,
Camouflaged, hidden and misplaced was I,
Away from my motherhood was I,
In a land distant from mines.

Earthborn as polite as I,
Accomplished my desire of life,
Providing me with endless cuisines.

I flew beyond the rollercoasters of rides,
I blended with the shines of lights,
I extended my view of life,

Without notice,
My eye, blinded my sight,
Nearby was my childhood, waiting for me.

Riya Maniz Carsane
Rushey Mead Academy, Leicester

A Journey Of Resilience

Through their eyes, I see him playing and yet trying
He has gone through many failures and discouragements
Sometimes filled with joy and sometimes crying, he made
Many wonderful achievements and still found hated

Through their eyes, I see a self-believing man
That has got many unwanted comments and being
Named a betrayer for money, he is one of the greatest
Batsmen that played for his nation, despite that, people still
Protest him.

Through their eyes, I see an all-rounder seeking for the great
Victory for his team and country, he is a player that no one
Imagined would do such a thing, but avoiding it he is
Still living his life happily.
Through their eyes, I see Hardik Pandya giving his most for the nation.

Dharmik Vipulbharti
Rushey Mead Academy, Leicester

Quack And Chaos

The duck goes quack
Am I under attack?

Large boats pass they're coming towards me!
Where do I go? I'm not that fast!

The water splashes, pushing me away...
I'm drifting further and further no wait!

There's a drop ahead, now I'm in trouble...
...all I can do is stumble and struggle

Why are there so many kids?
They look so happy but are they laughing at me?

Ahhhhh! I fall down the waterfall!
Uh-oh, watch out, I'm about to hit a wall!

Finally, the water's slow again
All of that for nothing, I was just doing my own thing!

Ava Chohan (12)
Rushey Mead Academy, Leicester

My Poem

We all grow up
Grow up so fast
From playtime
To study time
From a bright mind
To a dark mind
From enjoyment
To peace
From freedom
To overthinking
We all have our changes
From child
To adult.

Hate me
Love me
Do what you want with me
Anything you want
But there's a catch to it
If you think negative about me
Don't come and say it to me
If you think positive about me
Come say it to me
It'll make me smile
Not cry

You'd rather see someone smile
Than cry.

If you feel upset
Tell me
It's not fair if
We laugh together
But you cry alone.

Vaishnavi Purohit
Rushey Mead Academy, Leicester

The Thin Blue Line

Beep! Boop! My bodycam turns on
I run in, without a single care in the world
I have a duty to do
Care for my comrades
Take a bullet for them

I walk the thin blue line
My heart beats out of my chest
I am ready for this test

Wherever crime may be
I shall rush
I shall serve my duty

This uniform
This life
This vest
This Blue Line Badge

I shall not let you down
I ask for strength
I ask for courage
Strength and courage to help others

When something is wrong, report it right.

Tejvir Singh (12)
Rushey Mead Academy, Leicester

Being A Teenager

Being a teen was not fun
Acting like a teen was not fun
The stress and anxiety building up
I was scared

Being a teen was fun
Driving was fun
Being happy and going out was fun
Laughing and joking around was fun

Beauty
Am I ugly or am I pretty?
Beauty
They say I am pretty
I don't know to agree or not

Don't be scared
It's only a couple of years
Live your life, not other people's.

Reshmi Umasutharshan
Rushey Mead Academy, Leicester

Finding My Truth

Sometimes I dearly cry
Sometimes I simply sigh
Sometimes I feel as though I am too weak for this dreadful life
Sometimes I feel as though this world is not deserving of my puny tears
Yet
Sometimes I feel as though I am worthy of this lively land
Sometimes I feel as though I am worthy of this fierce life
Most times I turn a blind eye on these sickly lies, and cherish those faithful cries.

Hibba Nawfar (12)
Rushey Mead Academy, Leicester

Echoes Of My Soul

The hurt is true
The fight is real
My heart is gold
My bones are steel
As darkness engulfs my thoughts and my pride
The light runs away; far from sight
Who do I tell?
What do I say?
Questions run through my mind in disarray
"You aren't alone."
That's what they say
But do they understand the fear that is me?

Aaminah Mussa (12)
Rushey Mead Academy, Leicester

I Am A Little Voice

I am a little voice,
Who is trapped in a cave

"What is this room?
What is this place?"

The smirks and the laughter,
The points and the grins.
They gathered around me,
Prickling my skin.

I'm a little voice,
Who is trapped in its feeling,
The thin thread of joy,
The marks on the ceiling,

The sounds of the judgment:
It stood in one place,
Is stubborn like rocks,
Or ear-piercing pain.

I tried pushing through it,
I tried getting out,
But the cry of the scuttering sound,
Scared away the strength I've left.

We're two little voices,
Still being ignored.

The different options and choices,
Had drowned by the sound of the noise.

The sunshine, the happiness,
That fell out of sight,
That hid behind storms,
Of the grey clouds; so high.

We're five little voices,
We're quite on our way,
To the moment we looked for,
Through pain and the rain.

Through mountains, through leaves,
Through storms and the fields,
Through dirt and the mud,
And the big stream of fear.

We're ten little voices,
And we're nearly there.
Pushing through throngs,
Through judgment, despair.

We're strong and we're mighty,
We break through the stones,
We climb up the heights,
And shout at the noise.

We're all little voices,
But together we're one.

Alone we are frightened,
Side by side we are loud.

Sasha Glushkova (11)
Sawston Village College, Sawston

I Miss You

The world swirls around me.
My head is filled with gloom.
As I hear the story of my father.
The one who died too soon.
Someone is speaking but I'm not hearing.
The world is swaying but I'm not in the mood for playing.
The tears spill as the voice comes in clear.
The voice I never want to hear.
The voice who couldn't save my father.
The voice who tried to save my father.

Nothing could be helped.
Nothing could be done.
People could sob.
People could cry.
But nothing could be done,
To bring back who had left for the skies.
We still missed him though.
The father I lost.

Olivia Sayers (12)
Sawston Village College, Sawston

Remember

I don't remember my brother
Just sometimes when I'm playing
My thoughts rushing in my mind,
Cancelling out the sound of children
Only leaving me to hear the beeping
The beeping that held me by the neck in suspense
Waiting to know
If that was his last breath

I don't remember my brother
But when on a breezy autumn day
The gust from the morning weather
Rushing past me like the wind
Carried by the shouty doctors passing by
Against my face

I don't remember my brother
Only sometimes when zoning out
And daydreaming takes the best of me
Thinking about what and how many things
I could've done with him

I used to always get jealous of people with siblings
People who used to exaggerate the fights
They would get into with their sister
Or people who emphasized the words 'hate'

Or 'they are so annoying'
In the conversations, we would have

But I've learned to accept that
I've learned to grow past that
I've learned that jealousy
Is a normal part of being human
Of being me

But I always try to remember
To not use it to an advantage
Or let it take the best of me

Even though there are a few things
I cannot remember.

Mariam Boucetta (12)
Sawston Village College, Sawston

The Secret Life Of A Cat

In the day, a simple pet,
Sleeping cutely, breaking no sweat,
All fluffy, so cute, so small,
Yet at night, he conquers all!

He looks normal, this agile kitten,
But at night, his eyes glisten,
With power and might, Max is unique,
From head to tail, strong body physique.

A gentle pat, a slash of a claw,
He leaves all that watches in mesmerising awe.
Because Max is no ordinary feline,
As fast as light, as smart as Einstein!

A ninja, a hero, a superspy,
Call him what you want, but no one can deny,
A whiskered agent, fierce and sly,
A cloak of darkness in the sky

From rooftop high to alley low,
He gathers secrets no one can know.
From wall to wall, he ricochets,
A cunning, ruthless runaway!

Yet, at dawn, he comes back home,
Putting an end to his skilful roam.

For Max the cat, both fierce and free,
Lives two lives of secrecy.

A cute meow, a soft purr,
I pet his luscious fur.
He rolls and purrs on my lap,
And after work, he takes a long nap.

Timur Vedernikov (12)
Sawston Village College, Sawston

Empath

Can you hear it?
The screaming, all around
No voices only sounds

A fist grips my stomach,
A knife, to my heart.
I scream alongside
Because I cannot bear
Begging you to hear

No solution is given, and yet -
Is it not obvious?
Find them, follow the screams,
Don't let them suffer
And yet, some are deaf
To the cries
Of their own

I will help them
Alone
If I must

Will you?

Elizabeth Hull (16)
Sawston Village College, Sawston

Dreamy Success

There are ambitions
That has to be greatly succeeding in your rightful decisions
Fantasising luxurious goods
That can never evanesce
One answer to all notions
"Success is at its peak,
To be accomplished nevertheless of disappointment"
But if failure ponders
It is not the answer to achievement so far
Aspire to be consistent and eagerly focused
Merely to know that daring dreams pave the way to firing fortunes in life.

Sterlin Sajan (15)
Sawston Village College, Sawston

The Streets

Lying in my bed, staring at the sky,
Rubbish here and everywhere, but here I shall lie,
Millions walk past me, pretending I'm not here,
Hearing all the arguments, saying this world isn't sphere!

A tear rolls down my cheek, but I get up,
A river nearby, I need water, I check my bag, no cup,
The scenic view is traffic, and traffic it will stay,
The golden leaves crunching with every step I take,

The ground as uneven as a camel's humps,
Tripping over, on the floor, there's laughing, what a dump,
Sickness bugs travel round, I'm coughing non-stop,
No one even thinks to get me something from a shop,

Family are invisible, so are my friends,
I'm praying every day, when will this end,
A 12-year-old girl doesn't deserve this life,
She shouldn't have to sleep amongst the wildlife,

The life without a home is harder than you think,
But you don't care, sat on your couch of perfect pink,
Please come and help a little girl like me,
I need to go home and finally feel free.

Esmee Rowe
Swanmore College, Swanmore

The Sleek Cat

She pads across, and moves so sleek,
Hops up to the window and takes a peek.

When she jumps, when she lands,
Her paws don't make a single sound.

She sees the stars, the moon so bright,
A deep, dark hue, the sky tonight.

They seemed so pointed, her delicate ears,
Then they twitch, every time she hears.

Was it a twig? Did it snap?
Had someone stepped on it, or made it crack?

Then she listens, hears a rustle.
She doesn't move, not even a shuffle.

But now her legs hurt, and they start to ache.
No matter how hard she tries, she just can't stay awake.

She rotates her body, and starts heading back.
Slower and slower, her energy lacks.

She jumps through the window, and lands on her legs,
Sleepily pads over, and climbs into bed.

What will she dream about, robins and crows?
Is that what cats really do? Well, nobody knows.

Eden O'Dwyer (12)
Swanmore College, Swanmore

Fluttering Flowers

F lowers dance around me in the warm spring breeze
L ilac petals blow far away from me
U nder tall tree branches and over the crystal river
T wisting and turning under the sun, I wish this went on forever
T hough I am still sat there, as lonely as can be
E verybody's having fun except me.
R ight now starts to fall, dropping my fading green leaf
I nside I'm unhappy, outside I act fine
N ow people walk over me, treading me into the grass
G oing on their way, they don't acknowledge me as they pass

F orever I'm uncared for, just left here to rot
L ittle, people care for me, most people do not
O ther than being ruined, I have little to do
W hat can I do to be less let down?
E verything just makes me frown
R ather than sitting in sorrow
S ometimes I hope for a better day tomorrow.

Georgina Stafford (12)
Swanmore College, Swanmore

Miami

It's lights out, and away we go.
The drivers get away well, as fast as electro,
But a 24-year-old Lando Norris,
Sits in P6, not seeing much of his

Insane skill and determination,
Into turn 1, the curbs cause vibrations,
Around his whole car, but then he remembers,
A very cold night in November

On the 13th, 1999,
Put in this world to be as fierce as a canine,
He knew when he was young, he wanted to kart,
Just to fit in, just wanted to be a part

Of the Hall of Fame, with his own special story,
He wanted the trophy and to earn the glory,
He kept progressing his way up through the cars,
Now he is in Miami F1, and he isn't far

From winning his first Grand Prix after so many podiums,
Was this ending going to be utopian?
He came round the final corner and over the line,
Lando has landed, the main headline.

Wills Illman (13)
Swanmore College, Swanmore

Blue

I felt so blue when I woke up.
5:30, my clock said.
I stretched, I yawned. I rubbed my eyes.
I did not want to leave my bed.

I felt so blue on my drive to work.
I left my coat at home.
Outside was so cold and dark.
I couldn't help but feel alone.

I felt so blue walking into work.
I could not go home until late.
I would have to stay and work away,
Until the clock hit half-eight.

I felt so blue seeing all the patience,
The ones who were upset and in pain,
The ones waiting for sick loved ones,
Who they may never see again.

Another nurse caught my eye,
Pushing a hospital bed.
The patient in the bed was unresponsive,
"Code blue," the flustered nurse said.

Then I turned to the window behind me.
The ambulance lights flashed so bright.

And I was in a sea of blue.

Natalie Hadfield (13)
Swanmore College, Swanmore

Refugees Are Allowed

R eaching out for my parent's hand
E erie smoke blocking my view
F leeing to safety
U nderstanding nothing about this world
G rowling wind like the air from a fan
E xhausted, my eyes shut, not seeing anything but blackness
E veryone shouting around me, like a herd of elephants
S hivering is all I see

A honk from a boat far away
R aging and eager is all I feel
E xperienced everything

A ll is dark inside my heart
L unging forward into the crowd
L ifting myself off the ground
O pen up to this universe
W hen I see them, I will run
E verything is dull
D iving into the boat, I see them!

Lucy Barnes (13)
Swanmore College, Swanmore

Barbie

Everyone says that I have perfect, silky, blonde hair,
Everyone says that I have sparkly, stylish clothes,
Everyone says I have a perfect body that people would die for,

I feel like my hair is too hard to keep up and I can't be bothered anymore,
I have to waste all my money on new clothes every week,
I spend all my free time exercising until I can't walk anymore,

Everyone says I have glossy lips,
Everyone says I have flawless, glass skin,
Everyone says I have so many friends,

I have spent thousands on lip fillers,
I do hours of violent skin rituals,
I feel like all my friends hate me and are fake,

Everyone says my life is perfect,
But it's not at all.

Eve Shuker (12)
Swanmore College, Swanmore

Refugees Are Human

R efugee is what I am.
E ager to find my parents and,
F leeing to safety.
U need to go home!
G et away from here!
E xclaimed the man.
E xhausted, I just want to be safe.
S urrounded by piercing screams,

A human, that's all I want to be.
R estless, hungry, alone, that's all I am.
E veryone doesn't understand.

H umans, we are humans!
U nderestimated ordinary people,
M aking our way to safety.
A refugee, that's all you are.
N o! I will not just be a refugee.
S ee me for who I truly am!

Daisy Edwards (13)
Swanmore College, Swanmore

Don't Be Afraid

I started as a match.
Only a match.
I was struck against the box.
That was how I was awoken.
Don't be afraid.

I began to rise.
Higher, higher, higher.
Higher than ever.
Like never before.
You could have seen me for miles.
Don't be afraid.

People were running.
People were screaming.
But why?
Why from me?
Don't be afraid.

As I carried on moving.
I came to water.
My end.
Or new beginning.
Flowing in the wind I
entered the cold, frosty water.
I was gone.
Don't be afraid.

Now I rise into the sky.
But this time, not as hot as before.
Now I was steam.
Don't be afraid.

Fred Jarman (12)
Swanmore College, Swanmore

All Of My Wrong

Seven years ago
Owen went to play
But he never came back
In the woods, he must lay

Nobody could find him
Nobody but me
People are so blind
Oh, can't you just see?

Six years ago
They knew it was I
I said it was me
Why would I lie?

Five years ago
They let me free
Grace went missing
They knew it was me

Four years ago
They found her lying
I watched her family
I watched them crying

Three years ago
I finally stopped

Two was enough
But maybe it was not

One year ago
My twins were gone
I knew it was revenge
For all of my wrong.

Ella Harrison (13)
Swanmore College, Swanmore

The Cusp Of Life Or Death

Sitting anxiously, waiting those two years, oh so tough,
I waited, heart racing, for the Nazis to turn away.
My home destroyed, so battered, bruised and so rough,
I crept like a mouse, would I survive another day?
Relief ran through my stiff, broken body,
I had made it so nearly a year, as the blossom sprung, I quickly realised it was May.
Darkness surrounding me as I continued to hope,
I wondered where my family could be, happy, dead, alive, maybe they just forgot me.
It was life and death, would the evil cut the rope.
As the killers came to check on me, I was scared, would it be death? Or after two years, would I be free?

Henry Ainsworth (13)
Swanmore College, Swanmore

War

I started when a conflict occurred between two nations,
I am not a good omen for these countries' relations,
I am scared that I have broken some important laws,
I am scared for them too, the trouble I will cause,
I am destructive and conflicting, they are the qualities
I possess,
This proves that I am a nuisance, I am trying to confess,
To you, I am a sign of worry and despair,
As I am sure most of you are aware,
I am ashamed to admit all the people I've killed,
You could, in fact, say that I am quite skilled,
I wrote this to say that I am not thrilled,
That some of your lives will not be fulfilled,
Because of war.

Jack Cornwell
Swanmore College, Swanmore

A Waiting Pet

I am a dog, a cat, a fish, as happy as can be.
But when my human leaves for work, I am no longer glee.
The absence of my favourite person is not a good thing.
I am so tense and not at ease. I wish the door would ring.

Scratching at the door, making bubbles of rage.
I really dislike being trapped in this cage.
Come home now, I don't know what I'll do.
I really loved the times I've spent with you.

Playing fetch with my favourite ball.
On your lap, where I would sprawl.
Swimming round my tank with your eye on me.
I love you, owner, that I guarantee.

Teddy Turner
Swanmore College, Swanmore

I Wish

I wish she was here,
I wish I had told her,
I wish with all my heart I had known her.

I wish I'd had the courage,
I wish I'd had the strength,
I wish with all my heart that she had known.

Why didn't I tell her?
Why don't I know her?
Why didn't I ask when I had the chance?

If only I could go back in time and tell her,
If only I could go back in time and not have left her,
If only.

I wish she hadn't left,
I have so much to tell her,
Why did I wait so long to go up to her?

I miss her,
I need her,
I wish with all my heart I had known her.

Erin Wade (13)
Swanmore College, Swanmore

A Teenage Girl's Smile

I'm sat on my bedroom floor,
there are tears in my eyes,
I dread the knock at the door,
caught with surprise.

I roll down my sleeves,
wipe away my pain,
mirror, fake it please,
ignore the pain.

Act okay,
don't let them see,
go and play,
smile with glee.

I know it's hard, love,
but find the strength,
your heart's struggling self-worth,
look in the dark, you can make the length.

You wanna join the stars,
take away the yearning,
girl be proud of your scars,
we are just learning.

Chloe Pollard (14)
Swanmore College, Swanmore

JK Rowling

She sat there with barely enough money for some tea,
As at her side, her baby daughter smiled in her sleep.
She sighed and began to think back to her past,
No mother, no job and money that would not last.
With pen in hand, an idea began to form in her head,
What if this hobby became a career instead?
As she sat there, her past twirled into inspiration,
About a young wizard who went to school at King's Cross Station.
This is an idea that would grip the nation!
It could easily become an outstanding creation!
She beamed in delight - and began to write.

Evie Cornwell
Swanmore College, Swanmore

City Style

I walk through this place and I am calm,
I know this place like the lines on my palm,
I finally found where I belong,
It may be busy but you can hear the bird song,
This place is all about pretty fashion,
But luckily, that is my wildest passion,
I love the city although it is cold,
It is my life to control,
On every corner, there is a new shop,
And some may be a bit over-the-top,
This place can change you in many ways,
For me, it only took a few days,
The schools, the dramas might be the most famous thing,
But the songs keep the popularity tied on a string,
I am so very happy this place is part of my life.

Rosie Smith (12)
Swanmore College, Swanmore

Doctor, Doctor

The doctor says we are going to die,
If our cholesterol is too high.

There is mercury in the fish we fry.
Air pollution is now at an all-time high.

Our ground is full of toxic waste.
The waters now have a murky base.

Our favourite foods are full of chemicals.
Our cities are full of scattered, dirty landfills.

Much acid rain is pouring down.
Clear rivers are suddenly turning brown.

So believe me now, see your doctor, they are in.
But it won't matter. Death will soon win.

Beth Ashford
Swanmore College, Swanmore

Suffer Now Or Forever Hold Your Peace

When will my misery end?
The shrubbery burns beneath me like my temper.
Getting closer by the second.

I can't hold up my fight much longer.
My surroundings became unrecognisable.

Leaping flames danced towards me.
The flames are furious, but with passion.
Blazes of orange fill my eyes.

Dangerous flames sizzle like bacon.
Smouldering, flickering at my bark.
I was becoming charred.
Engulfed like the grassy fields in the distance.
I guess this is when we say our goodbyes.

Molly Creese (13)
Swanmore College, Swanmore

Troy Bolton

Tick. Tok. Tick. Tok.
Only 10 minute left
Tick. Tok.
My father's eyes looked at me in fear
Tick. Tok. Tick. Tok.
Everything went silent
As I was feeling overwhelmed
I was ready to give up
Tick. Tok. Tick. Tok.

I looked at my friends who are like family
to me
Tick. Tok. Tick. Tok.
Everything went blurry
Only 5 minutes left
And the last time we'll ever play as a team
Tick. Tok.
They passed the lightning ball to me
4 minutes left kept repeating in my head
As I scored the winning basket
Everyone cheered.

Olivia Evans (13)
Swanmore College, Swanmore

From Fire To Life

I am fire, I am death
I am a fiery hole to hell
I am apocalypse breath
Yet in time, I bring life

I am destruction yet I'm lasting
I'm carnage, extinction, loss
I'm the Earth's natural weaponry
But my ash feeds farms

I kill thousands every year
Just look at Vesuvius
I made the loudest sound ever
Whilst destroying an island

I am fire, I am death
Everything dies in the end
You have time before Yellowstone
Live life whilst you can.

William Cloud (13)
Swanmore College, Swanmore

They'll Lose Me

I miss the way I used to be,
Full of energy and life,
Since they came along, they've changed me,
But not for the better,
They dump their problems, their pain and their rubbish in me,
They know the pain they cause,
However, they continue,
I meant to be full of life,
Meant to be beautiful,
Calming, relaxing,
But instead, they walked down the beach,
With disgust spread on their faces,
As they chuck their waste,
Into my bright blue seas,
I hope they change,
I hope they fix me,
But before I lose hope, or else they'll lose me.

Emmy Mooney (12)
Swanmore College, Swanmore

A Soldier From Ukraine

I am a soldier
From Ukraine.
I am feeling scared
Because all around me,
I see
Wounded civilians
And my friends.
In my dreams,
What will happen
Is likely not soon.
As the situation is getting worse
And worse.
But I hope that soon
It will stop
And we will live
The way we lived before.
Before the war
With the Russian Federation.
More precisely
Before 2014.
I want to change the situation
That is happening
Around us
Now.

Yesya Shyshlevska (11)
Swanmore College, Swanmore

Harry Styles

I look out on the crowd, so full,
They scream with joy and my heartstrings pull,
A flicker of light as the torches glisten,
Dancing and singing, eager to listen,
The tech team shout, that's my cue,
Thousands sing along, "I love you!"
I still remember my first concert,
Me and the band in our black T-shirts,
I was so nervous, I almost couldn't do it,
I still am, I hate to admit it,
I learned a lesson. Give things a try.
Swallow your fear. Wipe your tears.
Dream big, play that gig.

Emily Berrow (12)
Swanmore College, Swanmore

Homelessness

You say I look happy
You say I look free
But you don't understand
The way you overlook me

You think you're a hero
Putting 5p in my cup
But let's both be honest
That won't buy me much

You think I'm a bad person
I promise I'm not
But I'm telling you now
I won't ask for a lot

A roof over my head
It could be something small
I don't need too much
I'm used to sleeping against a wall.

Seren Anthony (12)
Swanmore College, Swanmore

Messi

M y hard work has paid off, moving from Argentina to Barcelona, Spain, at 13 to become the best player ever.
E ven from the setbacks of when I was young, I kept on going.
S eeing the fear in the opposition's eyes, ready to majestically destroy the team.
S eeing the ball come to me, remaining calm. Defenders running at me, still calm. I majestically make them fall over.
I kept going when times were hard. So can you. It paid off for me, why not for you?

Lewis Carter (12)
Swanmore College, Swanmore

Different Views, Different Thoughts, Different Lies

Through their eyes,
the experience of a child is different.

You are a child.
Your parent is in another room.
Imagine it's your mother,
and she is crying.

Imagine your father is nowhere to be seen,
But when you ask, you're told, "Don't worry about a thing."

Children's minds are beautiful,
their emotions fragile too,
but when they learn the reality,
they mature, just like you.

Lily Ashman (12)
Swanmore College, Swanmore

There Is Hope

There is panic in the air.
There is smoke everywhere.
What shall I do?

There is panic in the air.
There is smoke everywhere.
Is there anywhere to go?

There is panic in the air.
There is smoke everywhere.
Let's get on a boat!

There's panic in the air.
There's smoke everywhere.
We need to go!

There is panic in the air.
There is smoke everywhere.
There is always hope!

Lilly
Swanmore College, Swanmore

Husband, The Baby And Me

The baby in my arms,
watching my husband be left behind,
with a cross charm in my hand,
to keep us safe from bombs,
tears all down his face,
cold shivering,
the train will carry us away,
but where to?

The baby in my arms,
she cries,
shh, my baby,
Daddy's going to be alright.

Bombs, bombs, and more bombs,
I hope this madness stops.
Where do they come from?
They come down quicker than rain,
at least we're safe upon this train.

Georgia April (13)
Swanmore College, Swanmore

A Lost Soul

My age is small,
A number between 13 and 15, that's all,
My hair gets pulled,
My friends, my family, they all get fooled,
Abuse, I try, I try, I plead, I refuse,
Abuse, abuse,
Why can't I call a truce?
Scar here, scar there,
But where's my saviour, my guardian, my guide?
They're there, nowhere
My energy is gone, no fight, no flight, not a single drop in sight.
How do you know what people are going through?
Ask, it takes time.

Taylor Oosthuizen (12)
Swanmore College, Swanmore

In My Eyes

In my eyes, I lie alone, all squished up against the cold
No defence against my own, I sit here feeling alone
I sleep here in fear, on here, the cold bare path
I wept and wept and cried and cried, but there was
Nothing on the inside, left alone, so lonely, I cried
No one, it was just me here, living in fear
I wish and wish that I wasn't here
And all of these feelings kept on bleeding...
Here alone... in my eyes.

Caitlin-Rose Rappini
Swanmore College, Swanmore

Now I Believe Them

I heard the banging,
Then the clanging,
The crackle from the TV,
They said it wouldn't be easy,
And now I believe them.

The guns were fired,
Aren't they getting tired?
Drinking dirty water from a cup,
They said they wouldn't give up,
And now I believe them.

Lying in my bed,
Resting my head,
Soldiers screaming, *"They're in here!"*
They said I'd live in constant fear,
And now I believe them.

Evie Carter (12)
Swanmore College, Swanmore

Blackbird

Blackbird, blackbird, what have you seen
gazing down at me?
A mother and her baby going for a stroll,
Look at how the pram wheels roll.
Blackbird, blackbird, what do you see?
A town moody as can be.
Blackbird, what can you see?
An adult working for their family.
Blackbird, what do you see?
Little old woman with her grandbabies.
Blackbird, what do you see?
Blackbird?
What did you see?

Mariella Osborne (12)
Swanmore College, Swanmore

Sabre Norris

S ockie, Biggy, Naz
A lways getting what I never had
B uying them all I ever wanted
R eally it should all be mine
E specially since I'm the oldest

N az is the worst
O ften we fight
R egretting what we've said soon after
R ecently she has become a mini me
I thought it was sweet at first but now it's not
S top.

Jessi Bicknelle-Kendall (13)
Swanmore College, Swanmore

The Life Of A Football

Getting whacked and smacked isn't great,
Hearing screams and shouts saying, "Don't drop back, mate!"
This is the life of a football.

Flying into the great big net,
Being rolled about when it's soaking wet,
This is the life of a football.

Winning the league with pride and joy,
Getting in the team photo with the big boys,
Maybe being a football isn't too bad.

Arthur Naysmith (11)
Swanmore College, Swanmore

The Mighty Mountain

I was a mighty mountain,
With fast rivers and tall peaks,
But then there came the people,
They cut me with their streets,
They covered me with houses,
And stabbed me with their steel,
And then I cried, I wept and wept,
My life did not feel real.

I was not a mighty mountain,
I had a broken face,
So when it comes to Earth's destruction,
Humans are always first place.

Thomas Oates (12)
Swanmore College, Swanmore

The Politician's Issues

Cruel world, existing.
Children crying, exhausting.
Corrupted by bribes, corrupting.
Chastised by naysayers, annoying.
Common men denying facts, tiring.
Courthouse lies, perjuring.
Chosen by peers, so trusting.
Chaos everywhere, volatile and unceasing.
Choosing his future, worrying.
Can't have his own opinion, damning.
Carved into a desk, his name and ink, drying.

Hayden Buckman (12)
Swanmore College, Swanmore

Saviour

Here I am again,
Searching for life,
Searching for shelter,
Searching for saviour.

Gruesome gas filled the air,
Deadly as any could imagine,
Looking and scouting,
Searching for saviour.

Deadly destruction struck the city,
Bombs as loud as thunder,
Desperately hoping,
Searching for saviour.

Why cry?
Why die?
Let's make peace and stop people,
Searching for saviour.

Noah Sumner (12)
Swanmore College, Swanmore

Let It Rain

I brush it off, bottle it up,
I'm turning grey, ready to burst,
But I can't, not while the sun is shining,
Not while the people are happy.

So I bottle it up,
Try to relax,
Dancing around in the sky,
I let it be.

But I've bottled too much up,
I'm violently turning grey,
I feel the rain slowly slipping,
Through every inch of me,
I let myself go,
I let it rain!

Ruby Webb
Swanmore College, Swanmore

Nobody's Perfect

Pink goes with everything, although my feelings don't,
I try to let it out but I can't, I won't,
You don't know my feelings and I hope you never will,
These dark and dingy thoughts of death may serve you an endless chill,
My bright blue eyes, which look like they've never cried,
Along with my pearly white teeth, I show,
Please just know I'm never smiling on the inside.

Annabel Phillips (12)
Swanmore College, Swanmore

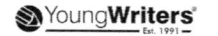

Through The Eyes Of A Worrier

Through every person who has ever lived, I have left a stain,
I don't mean to cause all the upset and pain,
I am a mix of you, past, present and future,
I don't mean to be a constant blooper,
I only was created by you,
By your thoughts and what you believed was true,
I am made to be left behind,
But I make contentment and more, satisfactory to find.

Eva Bowyer (12)
Swanmore College, Swanmore

Float Away

Parts of me float away,
I'm starting to decay,
It's lonely to be a piece of ice,
Yet I'm still a home for millions of lives,
It's hard to keep them alive,
Whilst no one hears my silent cries,
Now it's getting too warm,
Polar bears start to swarm,
Flowers start to bloom,
And I'm feeling quite gloom,
I won't die today,
But millions of lives will soon float away...

Teagan Callaghan (13)
Swanmore College, Swanmore

Escape

I wake from my sleep,
hearing the fearful shriek.
My sisters cry when they come.

Once again, we leave our home,
leaving behind all we own.
We run away, hoping to be safe,
but the war, so brutal, we must escape.

Our country, Ukraine, has been overrun,
we mustn't come back until the war is won.
Transported, I am, to Poland,
but my mother and sister, left behind.

Tessa Adkins (12)
Swanmore College, Swanmore

The Tree

There, the young tree stood,
Full of life and strength,

Two children played in the grass,
Giggling and stumbling around with glee,
The tree smiled happily,

The sound of a snap,
As his family were cut down,
What cruel people,
Oh, what a sound,

There the tree stood,
Its eyes full of tears,
What a cruel life,
It had only been years.

Abigail Wilkinson (12)
Swanmore College, Swanmore

I Hate My Life

I see people happy to see me
Because I got my tour today
Today I'm singing Vampire.

Everyone is going crazy
People never go this crazy to see me, never get a ticket.

It goes crazy when I'm singing
But when I'm not singing
They'll hate me, I feel sad and alone when I'm not singing.

Scarlett Beech (12)
Swanmore College, Swanmore

The Point Of No Return

We are at the point of no return
Light shakes its head at you
Now do you regret your decision?
Well, that's too bad
You've crossed the horizon
Prepare, for you will travel for millions of lightyears
Through a neverending tunnel
What would otherwise be impossible
We are past the point of no return.

Mia Thomas (13)
Swanmore College, Swanmore

Orangutan

I am locked up in a cage,
Eating nothing but mouldy sage,
Prying eyes stare scarily,
As my owner is beating me,
I do not know my own age,
I am locked up in a cage.

I was taken from my home,
Only so I can be shown,
My parents were killed by poachers,
How I watched by random approachers,
I arrived in a van,
I am an orangutan.

Thomas Grealy (13)
Swanmore College, Swanmore

Through The Eyes Of The Homeless

People stroll by me
Light in their eyes
I will never be them
I could never even try
A mother goes past
Her son in her arms
She prays that he will never
End up like me
A man reaches into his pocket
Flicks a coin into my hat
I thank him for trying
But it's never enough.

Delilah Hatcher
Swanmore College, Swanmore

The Fridge Life

People only like me when I'm full,
This is all,
When I'm empty, no one likes me,
That's not all, people don't know about me,
When it's dark and hopeless inside,
All the demons come alive,
It's like they give me loads of power,
But it only lasts about an hour.

Theo Southall
Swanmore College, Swanmore

Perfect Life

Through their eyes
Everyone wishes to be me.
Through their eyes
I'm as perfect as can be.
Through their eyes
I live the perfect life.

Through my eyes
I wish I was different.
Through my eyes
I hate how I look.
Through my eyes
I hate myself.

Harry Teague (13)
Swanmore College, Swanmore

Taylor Swift

T rauma
A lways having people following you around
Y oung but an amazing singer
L over album
O n task
R esilience

S inger
W orks hard
I nvincible
F earless album
T our.

Isabelle Booth (12)
Swanmore College, Swanmore

Planet Destroyer

Planet destroyer,
environment wrecker,
life's reaper,
self-destructor,
reckless invader,
conflict inducer,
atmosphere ripper.

A tyrant in a once peaceful world,
I am the human mind.

Wilfred Hammond (13)
Swanmore College, Swanmore

Left Unspoken

Scarred for life
Tired, even exhausted
Silenced from violence
You need to leave
Fight for what's right
I need a second chance
I'm broken and my words are left
Unspoken.

Matilda Horn (13)
Swanmore College, Swanmore

Violence

Gun shooter,
Ration eater,
Rain falls,
Loud bangs,
Sleep needer,
Uniform fixer,
Enemy slayer,
Family misser,
I am a WWII soldier.

Seth Henderson (11)
Swanmore College, Swanmore

Soldier

Anxious fighter.
Home misser.
Grave digger.
Jeep fixer.
Enemy slayer.
Peace maker.
Rations eater.
I'm a WWII soldier.

Ezri Hosking (12)
Swanmore College, Swanmore

Plug

Sometimes my life is boring,
Stuck in the same old place,
I get pushed and prodded,
I'm only noticed when you want me,
It often makes me mad,
Like I want to retaliate,
But there is only one problem...
I'm a plug socket.

Emily Pidduck
The Commonweal School, Swindon

I Am A Leaf

I am a leaf
With a story to tell,
Of how I grew, and lived, and fell,
Of friends I made along the way,
Although none of them could stay.

So light!
So bright!
Green is all around,
And to my ears is brought,
A gentle rustling sound.

Suddenly, I see
Someone looking at me,
Someone colourful,
Someone different,
A blossom.

We talked for a while,
How she made me smile!
Then when it reached the afternoon,
She said, "I will have to go soon."

Turning around,
I watched as my friend
Drifted slowly to the ground,
It felt like the end
But then my branch started to bend.

I saw a flash of red before my eyes,
It took me a moment to realise,
And then I looked in surprise,
For there on the branch below me was...
An apple.

The apple was funny,
The weather was sunny,
But one day I awoke to find,
That yet again, I had been left behind.

So light!
So bright!
Orange is all around,
And to my ears is brought,
A gentle rustling sound.

Then came a roaring, whistling sound,
That plucked me off my branch
And dragged me to the ground,
Twisting, twirling, turning,
Floating, flying, falling.

Oh, what a thrill!
Who would have thought it would
Fill someone with such joy,
Then came along a little boy,
Who picked me up and took me away.

I sat outside
And cried and cried,
How I missed my home so,
And then
It started to snow.

The wind picked me up,
Up, up, up, up, up, up,
And it blew me all over town,
Up, down, up, down,
I finally came to rest in a nest,
In my old tree!

I have learned a valuable lesson...

Things are lost,
Things are found,
But if you keep believing,
What goes around, comes around.

Molly Sargent (11)
The Commonweal School, Swindon

The Witch Hunter

Witch reports are on the rise
Scaring on brooms through the skies
So here's a lesson that I pitch
How to identify a witch.

Doth she own a pitch-black cat?
Doth she cause others to twitch?
Doth she don a pointed hat?
Hark! I declare, that she's a witch!

Doth she brew all kinds of potions?
Did her child become a snitch?
Doth she cause such a commotion?
Beware, thy neighbour is a witch!

Doth she spook you with a cackle?
Soar in the sky so high?
This demon we shall shackle,
And at the stake she'll fry!

Slams the door of a place so holy,
Enjoys berries so blue,
This is her purpose solely,
She's coming after you!

Luke Ireland (14)
Waterloo Lodge School, Chorley

Through The Eyes Of A Killer...

The stench of bodies twists around the room.
They were my fifth bait this time.
Depressed I am feeling.
The bodies crashed and splattered on my floor.
How many more bodies will occur?
How many lives will I take?
I'm a serial killer,
There's no mistake!

Hayleigh Carlos (15)
Waterloo Lodge School, Chorley

The Noble One

I am the noble one!
Everyone looks up to me!
And my fellow citizens, I look upon
Bow down to me, for I am the one!
I commission you to do as I say.
Learn from the wise and do not threaten,
For I am the noble one!

Jessica Hinton (15)
Waterloo Lodge School, Chorley

YoungWriters
Est. 1991

YOUNG WRITERS INFORMATION

We hope you have enjoyed reading this book – and that you will continue to in the coming years.

If you're a young writer who enjoys reading and creative writing, or the parent of an enthusiastic poet or story writer, do visit our website www.youngwriters.co.uk. Here you will find free competitions, workshops and games, as well as recommended reads, a poetry glossary and our blog. There's lots to keep budding writers motivated to write!

If you would like to order further copies of this book, or any of our other titles, then please give us a call or order via your online account.

Young Writers
Remus House
Coltsfoot Drive
Peterborough
PE2 9BF
(01733) 890066
info@youngwriters.co.uk

Join in the conversation!
Tips, news, giveaways and much more!

YoungWritersUK   **YoungWritersCW**
youngwriterscw   **youngwriterscw**